MIRACLE MEALS

Eight Nights of Food 'n Fun
for Chanukah

by Madeline Wikler and Judyth Groner
illustrated by Chari Radin

KAR-BEN COPIES, INC.   ROCKVILLE, MD

Library of Congress Cataloging-in-Publication Data

Groner, Judyth Saypol.
  Miracle meals.

  Summary: Presents instructions for preparing Hanukkah meals and suggestions
for games and party activities.
  1. Hanukkah cookery—Juvenile literature. 2. Hanukkah—Juvenile literature.
[1. Hanukkah cookery. 2. Hanukkah] I. Wikler, Madeline, 1943-0000. II. Radin,
Chari, ill. III. Title.
TX724.G726   1987   641.5′676435   87-17325
ISBN 0-930494-71-7

Some of the recipes and party ideas in this book previously appeared in Let's Have a
Party, *by Ruth Esrig Brinn with Judyth R. Saypol, and* My Very Own Jewish Calendar
by Judyth Groner and Madeline Wikler © Kar-Ben Copies, Inc.

CONTENTS

WELCOME! 4
USING THIS COOKBOOK 5
EQUIPMENT 6
THE STORY OF CHANUKAH 7
LIGHTING THE CANDLES 8
SOUPS 9

E-Z Chicken Soup 10   Lentil Soup 13
Chicken Soup 11   Minestrone Soup 14
E-Z Onion Soup 12

LOTSA LATKES 'N APPLESAUCE 15

E-Z Blender Latkes 16   Carrot Latkes 20
Crunchy Potato Latkes 17   E-Z Applesauce 21
Cheese Latkes 18   Chunky Applesauce 22
Apple 'n Cinnamon Latkes 19

DAIRY 23

Dreidel Sandwich 24   Pizza Bagels 29
Menorah Sandwich 25   Health Food Dreidels 30
Cheese Coins 26   Winter Fruit 'N Nut Salad 31
Candle Salad 27   Maccabee "Hero" Sandwich 32
Cheese Puff 28

MEAT 33

E-Z Latke Sandwich 34   Winter Stew 38
Hot Dog Kebabs 35   Meat Balls 39
Cornflake Chicken 36   Meat Loaf 40
Pot Roast 37

DESSERTS AND FUN FOODS 41

Candy Dreidels 42   Alef-Bet Pretzels 46
Snow Cream 43   Menorah or Dreidel Cake 47
E-Z Sufganiyot (Donuts) 44   Chanu-Cookies 48
Sufganiyot 45

DRINKS 49

Fruit Shake 50   Mulled Cider 53
Egg Cream 51   Punch 54
Hot Cocoa 52

CHANUKAH PARTIES 55

Candlelight Dinner 56   Pajama Party 58
Open House 57

CHANUKAH GAMES 59

Dreidel 60   Sufganiyot on a String 63
Dreidel Variations 61   Chanukah Gelt Treasure Hunt 64
Chanukah Bingo 62

WELCOME!

...to the first Chanukah cookbook just for kids. We've included enough recipes for eight days and nights of cooking adventures. There are five kinds of latkes, menorah sandwiches, candle salads, letter pretzels, a dreidel cake, and more. And if you want to have a Chanukah party, there are suggestions for themes, invitations, decorations, menus, and games. Happy Chanukah and happy cooking!

BEFORE YOU BEGIN...

- Ask permission to use the kitchen. If you are using sharp knives, the stove, or electrical appliances, make sure an older person is near to supervise.

- Wash your hands, and protect your clothes with an apron.

- Read the recipe carefully, and assemble all ingredients and equipment you will need. Clear a space to work, and keep a sponge handy for unexpected spills.

- Remember these safety tips:

    *Use potholders to handle hot dishes.

    *Turn pot handles toward the back of the stove, so you don't accidentally knock over a hot pot.

    *Pick up knives by the handle, not the blade, and always cut away from yourself.

    *Always wash fresh fruits and vegetables.

    *Every kitchen should have a portable fire extinguisher in an easy-to-reach place.

    *Never, ever, put out an oil fire with water. If you don't have a fire extinguisher, pour salt, baking soda, or flour on the fire to suffocate the flames.

- When you're finished, turn off the stove or oven, put away all food, and wash, dry, and put away all equipment. Wipe the counters, and sweep the floor. Remember, good cooks always leave the kitchen neat and clean.

USING THIS COOKBOOK

E-Z SYMBOLS

 means very easy. No cooking or baking is required. Cutting may be done with a plastic knife. Even your little brother can help.

 means you may have to chop, slice, use a blender or food processor, or bake. Depending upon your age, you may need supervision.

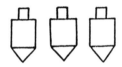 means you must use a hot stove to boil or fry. An adult should be present when you make these recipes.

MEAT/DAIRY/PARVE SYMBOLS

 is a meat recipe

 is a dairy recipe

 is a parve recipe (may be eaten with either meat or dairy).

If your family keeps a kosher home, it is important to use the correct dishes and pots in preparing your recipe. Sometimes a dairy dish can be made parve just by using parve margarine instead of butter. These recipes have the symbols D/P.

COOKING METRIC

Teaspoons to Milliliters
¼ tsp. = 1¼ ml
½ tsp. = 2½ ml
1 tsp. = 5 ml

Tablespoons to Milliliters
1 Tbsp. = 15 ml

Cups to Milliliters
¼ cup = 60 ml
½ cup = 120 ml
1 cup = 240 ml
4 cups (1 quart) = .95 liter

Ounces to Grams
1 oz. = 28½ gm
4 oz. = 114 gm
16 oz. (1 pound) = 456 gm

Fahrenheit to Celsius
250°F = 121°C
300°F = 149°C
350°F = 177°C
400°F = 204°C

Other Useful Equivalents
3 tsp. = 1 Tbsp.
4 Tbsp. = ¼ cup
8 oz = ½ pint = 1 cup
32 oz. = 4 cups = 1 quart

EQUIPMENT

Cooking goes faster when you have everything ready. Check the equipment list under the ingredients before you start each recipe. These pictures will help you find what you need.

 BAKING DISH

 BEATERS

 BOWL/PUNCH BOWL

 CAN OPENER

 COLANDER

 COOKIE SHEET

 CUTTING BOARD

 DISH TOWEL

 FOOD PROCESSOR OR BLENDER

 FRYING PAN

 GRATER

 LADLE

 MEASURING CUP AND SPOONS

 MUGS

 PAPER TOWEL

 PASTRY BRUSH

 PLASTIC WRAP

 PLATE

 POT

 POT HOLDER

 ROASTING/BAKING PAN

 SCRAPER

 SIFTER

 SLOTTED PANCAKE TURNER

 SPATULA

 SQUEEZE BOTTLE

 TIMER

 TOOTHPICKS

 VEGETABLE PEELER

 WAXED PAPER/ FOIL

THE STORY OF CHANUKAH

Long ago, the Jewish people lived in the land of Israel, then called Judea. They were ruled by the king of nearby Syria. Although they were not free, they were allowed to celebrate their holidays and pray in their Holy Temple in Jerusalem. But a new king, Antiochus, came to power. He forced the Jews to believe in the Greek gods, and to bow down to Greek statues. When some Jews refused, Antiochus sent soldiers to destroy the homes and Temple of the Jews.

In Modi'in, a town near Jerusalem, a man called Mattathias refused to bow down to the Greek statues. With his five sons, he fought off the soldiers and escaped to the nearby mountains. They organized a small army, called the Maccabees, led by Mattathias' son Judah. Though they were few in number, and not well-trained, the Maccabees were fighting for freedom, and their courage and skill enabled them to drive the Syrians away.

After three years of fighting, they reached Jerusalem. The Jewish fighters became builders, as they cleaned and rebuilt the Holy Temple. On the 25th day of the Hebrew month Kislev, they rekindled the lights of the menorah and rededicated the Holy Temple. Their celebration lasted eight days. Judah Maccabee and his brothers proclaimed that every year, for eight days, the Jews should celebrate a Festival of Lights. This holiday became known as Chanukah.

There is a legend that the Maccabees were able to find only one jug of pure oil, enough to keep the Temple menorah burning for only one day. But the oil lasted and lasted, and burned brightly for all eight days of the celebration.

As a reminder of the miracle of the oil, it is a Chanukah tradition to eat foods cooked in oil, such as latkes and donuts.

LIGHTING THE CANDLES

The Chanukah menorah, called the *chanukiyah*, should be lit at sunset and placed in front of a window, so that people passing by can see the candles burning. You need 44 candles for all 8 nights. Each night a *shamash* (helper) candle is lit and is used to light first one candle, then two, and so forth.

Candles should be lined up from right to left. The last candle added is the first one lit, and the lighting continues from left to right.

In some families, it is the custom for everyone to light his or her own *chanukiyah*. In other families, parents and children take turns. On Shabbat, light the Chanukah candles before the Shabbat candles.

CANDLE BLESSINGS

בָּרוּךְ אַתָּה יהוה אֱלֹהֵינוּ מֶלֶךְ הָעוֹלָם, אֲשֶׁר קִדְּשָׁנוּ בְּמִצְוֹתָיו וְצִוָּנוּ לְהַדְלִיק נֵר שֶׁל חֲנֻכָּה.

Baruch Atah Adonai Eloheinu, melech ha'olam, asher kid'shanu b'mitzvotav v'tzivanu, l'hadlik ner shel Chanukah.

We praise You, Adonai our God, Ruler of the World, who makes us holy by Your mitzvot, and commands us to light the Chanukah candles.

בָּרוּךְ אַתָּה יהוה אֱלֹהֵינוּ מֶלֶךְ הָעוֹלָם, שֶׁעָשָׂה נִסִּים לַאֲבוֹתֵינוּ בַּיָּמִים הָהֵם בַּזְּמַן הַזֶּה.

Baruch Atah Adonai, Eloheinu, melech ha'olam, she'asah nisim la'avoteinu bayamim hahem baz'man hazeh.

We praise You, Adonai our God, Ruler of the World, who made miracles for our ancestors in those days, in this season.

On the first night, we add a third blessing:

בָּרוּךְ אַתָּה יהוה אֱלֹהֵינוּ מֶלֶךְ הָעוֹלָם, שֶׁהֶחֱיָנוּ וְקִיְּמָנוּ וְהִגִּיעָנוּ לַזְּמַן הַזֶּה.

Baruch Atah Adonai, Eloheinu, melech ha'olam, she'hecheyanu, v'kiy'manu, v'higianu, lazman hazeh.

We praise You, Adonai our God, Ruler of the World, who has kept us alive and well so that we can celebrate this special time.

SOUPS

E-Z CHICKEN SOUP

What You Need:

4 chicken bouillon cubes
4 c. water
1 carrot
1 stalk of celery
½ tsp. dill

Pot with cover
Pot holder
Measuring cup and spoons
Vegetable peeler
Knife and cutting board
Timer

What You Do:

1. Put bouillon and water in pot, and bring to a boil. Turn down heat.

2. Wash, peel, and slice carrot and celery into ½ inch rounds, and add to soup. Add dill.

3. Cover and simmer until vegetables are soft (about 20 minutes).

   Serves 4

CHICKEN SOUP

What You Need:

8 c. water
1 chicken (about 3 lbs.) in parts
2 carrots
1 onion
4 celery tops with leaves
1 bay leaf
2 tsp. salt
1 tsp. pepper

Measuring cups and spoons
Pot and cover
Pot holder
Vegetable peeler
Timer
Spoon, Knife
Strainer
Storage containers

What You Do:

1. Put water in pot. Add chicken. Peel vegetables, and add to soup. Bring to a boil, lower heat, and simmer, covered, for 1½ hours until chicken is tender.

2. Remove chicken and vegetables. Strain soup into another pot or large jar. Cut carrots into pieces and return to soup. Refrigerate for several hours.

3. Remove layer of fat. Reheat soup to serve. Save chicken pieces for chicken salad.

Serves 10-12

E-Z ONION SOUP

What You Need:

1 package onion soup mix
4 slices of bread
4 slices of cheese
margarine

Knife
Pot and pot holder
Ladle
Serving bowls

What You Do:

1. Prepare onion soup mix according to package directions.
2. Spread margarine on bread, and top with slice of cheese. Toast on tray in toaster oven or oven.
3. Ladle soup into bowls. Put piece of melted cheese-toast on top.

   Serves 4

LENTIL SOUP

What You Need:

1 onion
1 lb. of chicken parts
2 Tbsp. oil
2 carrots
2 celery stalks
4 c. water
1-1 lb. can tomato juice
½ lb. lentils
1 tsp. salt
½ tsp. each garlic, pepper, and
  parsley

Knife and cutting board
Measuring cup and spoons
Pot with cover
Spoon
Vegetable peeler
Can opener
Pot holder, timer

What You Do:

1. Cut the onion in ½″ pieces. Put in pot with chicken and oil, and saute for 5 minutes. Stir occasionally.

2. Peel carrots. Cut carrots and celery into ½″ pieces, and add to pot.

3. Add water, tomato juice, lentils, and spices. Bring to a boil, lower heat, and simmer, covered for 1½ hours until lentils are soft.

Serves 8-10

13

MINESTRONE SOUP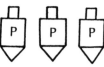

What You Need:

6 c. water
1 can tomato paste
1 can kidney beans
1 zucchini
2 carrots
1 onion
1 potato
1 c. cabbage
½ c. green beans
½ c. macaroni
1 tsp. salt
½ tsp. pepper
1 tsp. parsley

Can opener
Pot with cover
Pot holder
Spoon
Vegetable peeler
Knife and cutting board
Measuring cup and spoons
Timer

What You Do:

1. Put water and tomato paste into pot and stir. Bring to a boil, lower heat and simmer, covered, for ½ hour.

2. Peel and cut vegetables into ½ inch pieces, and add to pot. Simmer, covered, for another ½ hour.

3. Add macaroni and spices, and simmer for 15 minutes more.

Serves 8-10

LOTSA LATKES
'N APPLESAUCE

E-Z BLENDER LATKES

What You Need:

2 medium sweet or white
  potatoes (about 2 c. diced)
1 Tbsp. onion flakes
1 tsp. salt
1 egg
1 Tbsp. flour
½ c. oil for frying

Blender
Vegetable peeler
Knife and cutting board
Bowl and spoon
Frying pan and pot holder
Slotted pancake turner
Paper towel

What You Do:

1. Peel potatoes, and cut into 1" pieces. (You may scrub the potatoes well and use with skins if you wish.)

2. Put half the potatoes and rest of ingredients (except oil) in blender, and blend. Add rest of potatoes, and blend some more. Pour batter into bowl.

3. Heat 2 Tbsp. oil in frying pan. Spoon batter by tablespoonfuls into hot oil. Fry until brown around the edges. Turn and fry on the other side.

4. Drain on paper towel. Serve with applesauce or sour cream.

Serves 2-4

CRUNCHY POTATO LATKES

What You Need:

4 medium white or red potatoes (about 4 c. pieces)
1 medium onion (about ½ c. diced)
2 tsp. salt
2 eggs
2 Tbsp. flour
½ c. oil for frying

Knife and spoon
Food processor
Bowl
Measuring cup and spoons
Frying pan and pot holder
Slotted pancake turner
Paper towel

What You Do:

1. Peel potatoes, and cut into large pieces.

2. Shred potatoes in processor with medium shredder. Remove. Drain excess liquid.

3. Put steel blade in processor. Process onion. Add shredded potatoes, salt, eggs, and flour, and blend for a few seconds. Pour batter into bowl.

4. Heat 2 Tbsp. oil in pan. Spoon by tablespoonfuls into oil, and fry on one side until brown around the edges. Turn and fry on other side. Drain on paper towel.

Serves 3-4

CHEESE LATKES

What You Need:

1 c. ricotta cheese
4 eggs
⅔ c. flour
½ tsp. salt
2 Tbsp. margarine or oil for
   frying
Cinnamon and sugar

Measuring cup and spoons
Bowl
Fork and spoon
Frying pan and pot holder
Pancake turner
Paper towels

What You Do:

1. Put cheese and eggs in bowl and mix well.
2. Add flour and salt and mix again.
3. Heat oil or margarine in frying pan over medium heat.
4. Carefully spoon batter by tablespoonfuls into pan. Fry on one side until pancakes bubble. Turn and fry on second side until brown.
5. Drain on paper towel. Sprinkle with cinnamon and sugar.

Serves 3-4

APPLE-CINNAMON LATKES

What You Need:

1 egg
3 Tbsp. sugar
1 tsp. salt
1 tsp. cinnamon
⅓ c. water
3 c. chopped apples (about 3
   apples)
½ c. flour
½ c. oil for frying
½ c. sugar
1 tsp. cinnamon

Measuring cup and spoons
Bowl and mixing spoon
Blender or food processor
Vegetable peeler
Knife and cutting board
Frying pan and pot holder
Slotted pancake turner
Paper towels
Small bowl

What You Do:

1. In blender, beat egg until foamy. Add sugar, 1 tsp. cinnamon, salt, and water. Mix well.

2. Peel apples and cut into chunks. Add to egg a few at a time and blend.

3. Add flour and blend mixture until smooth.

4. Heat 2 Tbsp. oil in large frying pan. For each latke, spoon ¼ c. batter into hot oil. Fry until edges are brown. Turn and fry other side.

5. Remove with slotted pancake turner and drain on paper towel.

6. Mix remaining sugar and cinnamon in small bowl and sprinkle over hot latkes.

Serves 4-6

CARROT LATKES P P P

What You Need:

3 eggs
2 c. grated carrots (6-8 carrots)
2 c. bread crumbs
½ c. orange juice
1 tsp. cinnamon
½ tsp. salt
2-4 Tbsp. oil for frying

Bowl
Measuring cup and spoons
Fork, spoon
Vegetable peeler
Food processor or grater
Frying pan and pot holder
Pancake turner
Paper towels

What You Do:

1. Put eggs in bowl, and beat with fork.
2. Wash and peel carrots, and grate into bowl.
3. Add rest of ingredients, and mix well.
4. Heat oil in frying pan. Form batter into patties and fry on both sides until brown (about 3 minutes each side).
5. Drain on paper towels.

   Serves 4-6

E-Z APPLESAUCE

What You Need:

4 large apples
½ c. water
3 Tbsp. honey
1/8 tsp. cinnamon

Vegetable peeler
Measuring cup and spoons
Knife and cutting board
Bowl, spoon
Blender or food processor

What You Do:

1. Peel, core, and cut apples into large chunks.
2. Place in blender with rest of ingredients, and blend until smooth. You may have to blend half at a time, depending on size of blender or processor.
3. Serve immediately.

   Serves 4

CHUNKY APPLESAUCE

What You Need:

8 medium or 6 large apples
½ c. water
Dash of salt
½ c. sugar
½ tsp. cinnamon (optional)

Measuring cup and spoons
Pot with cover
Vegetable peeler
Knife and cutting board
Bowl, spoon
Pot holder
Timer

What You Do:

1. Pare and core apples. Put in pot with water and salt. Cover and cook over medium heat until apples are soft (about 30 minutes).

2. Add sugar and stir until sugar melts. Stir in cinnamon.

3. Transfer to bowl. Applesauce may be served warm or cold.

   Serves 6-8

DAIRY

DREIDEL SANDWICHES

What You Need:

Peanut butter (about ½ c.)
1 apple or banana
1 celery stalk
4 slices of whole wheat or other
　bread
1 carrot or half of a
　green pepper

Dish
Knife and cutting board

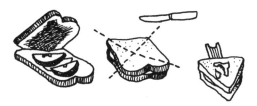

What You Do:

1. Spread the peanut butter on two slices of bread.

2. Slice the apple or banana into thin strips and put them on the peanut butter. Top with other two slices of bread.

3. Cut each sandwich in quarters diagonally. Cut celery into strips, and place one strip inside each triangle to make a dreidel handle.

4. Make dreidel letters with thin strips of green pepper or carrot, and attach to dreidel with peanut butter.

Makes 8

MENORAH SANDWICH

What You Need:

1 slice of bread
2 Tbsp. whipped cream cheese
8 small pretzel sticks
1 long thin slice of carrot or
celery
9 raisins

Plate
Vegetable peeler
Knife and cutting board

What You Do:

1. Spread cream cheese on bread.
2. Arrange pretzel stick "candles" and carrot stick "shamash" to make a Chanukah menorah.
3. Use raisins to "light" your menorah.

   Serves 1

CHEESE COINS

What You Need:

½ c. butter or margarine,
  softened
½ c. sharp cheddar cheese,
  shredded
1 c. flour

___

Measuring cup
Bowl and spoon
Waxed paper or plastic wrap
Cookie sheet and pot holder
Knife and cutting board
Timer

What You Do:

1. Combine all ingredients in a bowl. Mix well to form dough. Divide dough in half, and roll each half into a log. Wrap in waxed paper and chill or freeze for several hours or overnight.

2. Preheat oven to 375°.

3. Unwrap cheese logs, and slice into ¼″ coins. Place on ungreased cookie sheet an inch apart.

4. Bake for 10 minutes.

   Makes 3-4 dozen

CANDLE SALAD

What You Need:

2 lettuce leaves
½ c. cottage cheese
1 banana
2 slices of canned pineapple
2 slices of orange

Can opener
Measuring cup
Plates
Knife, spoon
Toothpicks

What You Do:

1. Put a lettuce leaf on each plate. Top with small mound of cottage cheese. Put a pineapple slice on top of the cheese.

2. Peel banana and cut in half. Place each half, cut side down, on salad. Fasten an orange slice to top of banana with a toothpick.

Serves 2

CHEESE PUFF

What You Need:

12 slices of white bread
6 slices of American cheese
1 stick butter or margarine,
  softened
3 eggs
3 c. milk
¼ tsp. salt
Paprika

Knife and cutting board
Baking dish
Bowl
Measuring cup and spoons
Fork or egg beater
Pot holder
Timer

What You Do:

1. Preheat oven to 325°.
2. Cut crusts off bread and butter each slice.
3. Grease baking dish with butter and place six of the bread slices in the dish, buttered side up. Cover each with a piece of cheese and top with remaining bread, buttered side up.
4. Beat eggs together with milk and salt. Pour into baking dish. Sprinkle with paprika.
5. Bake for 50 minutes or until puffy and brown.

Serves 6-8

PIZZA BAGELS

What You Need:

1 bagel
2 Tbsp. shredded mozzarella cheese
2 Tbsp. tomato sauce
¼ green pepper or 2 mushrooms (optional)
1 Tbsp. oil

Cookie sheet or toaster oven tray
Pastry brush
Measuring spoons
Knife and cutting board
Pot holder, timer

What You Do:

1. Preheat oven to 350°.

2. Slice bagel in half. Place on toaster tray cut side up. Brush with oil.

3. Spoon 1 Tbsp. tomato sauce onto each, and top with cheese and vegetables.

4. Bake 5 minutes until cheese bubbles.

Serves 1-2

HEALTH FOOD DREIDELS D/P

What You Need:

1 cucumber
3 radishes
3 olives without pits
3 cherry tomatoes
¼ lb. chunk of cheese

Knife and cutting board
Toothpicks
Plate

What You Do:

1. Cut cucumber and cheese into ¾"
   cubes to make dreidel bodies.

2. Cut olives, radishes, and cherry
   tomatoes in half. Attach with
   toothpicks to make dreidel spinners.

Makes 18

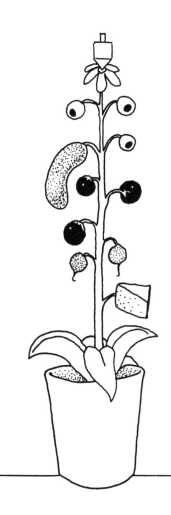

WINTER FRUIT 'N NUT SALAD

What You Need:

1 orange
1 banana
1 apple
1 pear
½ c. chopped nuts (optional)
1 fruit-flavored yogurt

_____

Bowl and spoon
Knife and cutting board
Blender

What You Do:

1. Peel orange and cut sections in half. Core apple and pear and cut into half-inch pieces. Peel banana and slice into quarter-inch pieces.

2. Combine in bowl with nuts (optional).

3. Blend yogurt until smooth. Pour over fruit salad just before serving.

Serves 2-3

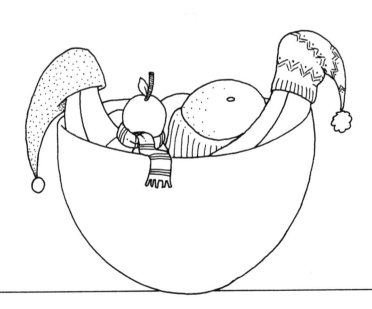

MACCABEE "HERO" SANDWICH

What You Need:

1 can tuna
1 Tbsp. mayonnaise
1 stalk celery
1 Italian or French bread roll
2 Tbsp. ketchup
1 Tbsp. mayonnaise

_____

Can opener
Bowl
Knife and cutting board
Spoon
Squeeze bottle

What You Do:

1. Put tuna and mayonnaise in bowl.

2. Cut celery into tiny pieces and mix with tuna.

3. Cut roll in half lengthwise, and scoop out middle. Fill roll with tuna salad.

4. Mix ketchup and mayonnaise, and pour into squeeze bottle. Use to give Judah a face and shield. Slice to serve.

Serves 2-3

MEAT

E-Z LATKE SANDWICH

What You Need:

1-2 frozen latkes for each
 sandwich
1-2 slices of salami, bologna, or
 roast beef

Cookie sheet and pot holder
Knife and cutting board
Fork, spoon
Timer

What You Do:

1. Bake latkes according to package
 directions.

2. Fill with meat.

3. You may make your sandwich "open
 face!"

Serves 1

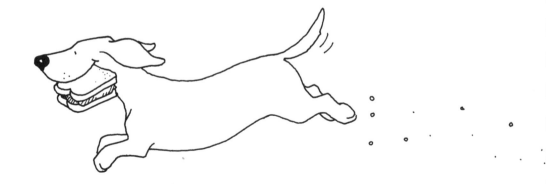

HOT DOG KEBABS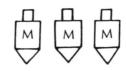

What You Need:

2 hot dogs
10 cherry tomatoes
2 pickles
Mustard and ketchup

Pot and pot holder
Timer
Knife and cutting board
Toothpicks

What You Do:

1. Put hot dogs in pot and cover with water. Bring to a boil and cook 3 minutes. Remove hot dogs and let cool for a few minutes.

2. Cut hot dogs and pickle in ½ inch slices. Cut cherry tomatoes in half.

3. Put a slice of hot dog, tomato, and pickle on each toothpick. Serve with ketchup and mustard.

Makes 20

CORNFLAKE CHICKEN

What You Need:

3 lbs. chicken parts
½ c. Italian dressing
1 c. cornflake crumbs

Paper towel
Bowl and spoon
Measuring cup
Paper or plastic bag
Baking dish and pot holder
Timer

What You Do:

1. Preheat oven to 350°.
2. Rinse chicken parts and pat dry.
3. Put chicken in bowl. Add salad dressing and mix. Marinate one hour.
4. Put crumbs in bag. Add chicken, two pieces at a time. Hold the bag closed, and shake to coat chicken.
5. Arrange pieces in single layer on baking dish. Bake for 1 hour.

Serves 4-6

POT ROAST M M

What You Need:

3 lbs. chuck, top rib, or other
  roast
1 package dried onion soup mix
½ c. ketchup
1 c. water

Measuring cup
Bowl and spoon
Covered frying pan or dutch
  oven
Pot holder
Timer

What You Do:

1. Place roast in pan, and brown over medium heat on both sides.

2. Mix onion soup mix, ketchup, and water in a bowl, and pour over meat.

3. Cover pan, and cook over low heat for 1½ hours.

Serves 6-8

WINTER STEW

What You Need:

2 lbs. beef or veal cubes
3 carrots
2 stalks celery
8 tiny red potatoes
1 slice challah or other parve
  bread
1-1 lb. can tomato sauce
1 can water
Salt, pepper, and garlic powder
  (optional)

Covered baking dish
Vegetable peeler
Knife and cutting board
Can opener
Spoon
Pot holder
Timer

What You Do:

1. Preheat oven to 350°.
2. Put meat in baking dish.
3. Peel and cut carrots and celery into 1″ slices. Add to meat.
4. Scrub potatoes and add to pot.
5. Cut challah into ½″ cubes and add to pot.
6. Add tomato sauce. Fill can with water, and pour over stew. Mix with large spoon.
7. Cover and bake for 2-3 hours.

   Serves 6-8

MEAT BALLS

What You Need:

1 lb. ground beef
1 Tbsp. dried, minced onion
flakes
1 egg
1 c. chili sauce
⅓ c. grape jelly
1 Tbsp. lemon juice

Bowl and spoon
Measuring cup and spoons
Pot with cover
Pot holder
Timer

What You Do:

1. Mix meat, onion flakes, and egg in a bowl.
2. Mix chili sauce, grape jelly, and lemon juice in pot. Form meat into balls the size of a walnut. Place in pot.
3. Bring to boil. Turn down heat, cover pot, and simmer for one hour.

Serves 4-6

MEAT LOAF

What You Need:

1 lb. ground beef
½ c. water
½ c. tomato sauce
½ c. breadcrumbs
1 egg
1 Tbsp. onion flakes
Salt, pepper, and garlic power
  (optional)

Bowl and spoon
Measuring cup and spoons
Loaf pan and pot holder
Timer

What You Do:

1. Preheat oven to 350°.
2. Mix all ingredients together in a bowl.
3. Pat into loaf pan.
4. Bake for 1 hour.

   Serves 4

DESSERTS
AND
FUN FOODS

CANDY DREIDELS

What You Need:

12 marshmallows
12 chocolate stars or kisses
Peanut butter
12 1″ long pieces of licorice or
    other candy stick
Food coloring

_____

Plate
Knife
Toothpick

What You Do:

1. Spread peanut butter on one flat side of marshmallow and attach chocolate kiss.

2. Poke the licorice or candy stick into the marshmallow for a handle.

3. Dip the toothpick in food coloring and paint a dreidel letter on the marshmallow.

SNOW CREAM

What You Need:

1 c. milk
¼ c. sugar
1 egg
1 tsp. vanilla or orange juice
  concentrate
Snow

Measuring cup and spoon
Bowl
Blender
Spoon

What You Do:

1. Put milk, sugar, egg, and flavoring in blender. Blend well.

2. Pour mixture in bowl.

3. Take outside, and add enough clean snow to absorb all liquid. Snow cream should be like soft sherbet.

Serves 4

E-Z SUFGANIYOT (DONUTS)

What You Need:

4 donuts
½ c. jam, jelly, peanut butter,
    softened ice cream, chocolate
    pudding, or whipped topping

Knife, cutting board
Spoon

What You Do:

1. Cut each donut in half.
2. Spread cut sides with fillings. Close
   to make donut "sandwiches."
   Serves 4

44

SUFGANIYOT (DONUTS)

What You Need:

½ c. orange juice
¼ lb. margarine
4 Tbsp. sugar
2 pkg. dry yeast
3-4 c. flour
2 eggs, beaten
Dash of salt
1 c. oil for frying
½ c. sugar

Measuring cup and spoons
Bowl and mixing spoon
Pot
Dish towel
Timer
Frying pan and pot holder
Plate and paper towels
Slotted spoon
Paper bag

What You Do:

1. Combine juice, margarine, and 4 Tbsp. sugar in small pot. Heat to melt margarine. Cool to lukewarm.

2. Add yeast, 3 c. flour, and beaten eggs. Knead until smooth, adding more flour if necessary.

3. Cover with damp dish towel and let rise 30 minutes.

4. Punch down. Divide into portions the size of a golf ball. Shape into balls, rings, or braids. Let rise 30 minutes more.

5. Heat 1 c. oil in frying pan. Fry donuts, turning to brown on all sides. Remove with slotted spoon and drain on paper towels.

6. Put ½ c. sugar in paper bag, and shake warm donuts to cover (optional). Serve warm.

Makes 12-14

ALEF-BET PRETZELS

What You Need:

1 package dry yeast
1 c. warm water
3 c. flour
1 Tbsp. sugar
1 tsp. salt
1 egg beaten with 1 Tbsp. water
Kosher or rock salt
Margarine

Bowl and spoon
Measuring cup and spoons
Dish towel
Timer
Small bowl and fork
Pastry brush
Cookie sheet
Pot holder

What You Do:

1. In a bowl, dissolve yeast in water. Add flour, sugar, and salt, and work into a dough. Cover with a towel and let rise 1 hour.

2. Preheat oven to 425°. Grease cookie sheet with margarine.

3. Divide dough into pieces the size of a golf ball. Dust hands with flour. Roll into sausages and shape into the letters on the dreidel. Place on cookie sheet, brush with egg, and sprinkle with kosher salt.

4. Bake for 25 minutes or until brown.

Makes 12-16

MENORAH OR DREIDEL CAKE

What You Need:

1 cake mix
1 pkg. frosting mix or 1 can of
  frosting
Orange or lemon candies

Bowl and spoon
Cake pan and pot holder
Cookie sheet or tray
Foil
Knife
Spatula
Timer

What You Do:

1. Prepare cake according to package directions. Bake in 9×13" pan.

2. Cool cake and remove from pan. Wrap in foil and freeze.

3. Remove from freezer and unwrap. Let cake thaw slightly while you prepare frosting.

4. Cut cake into pieces as shown, to make a dreidel or a menorah. Assemble pieces on cookie sheet or tray, and frost while cake is still partially frozen.

5. Use candy drops for candle flames on menorah or to make a letter on the dreidel.

Serves 8-10

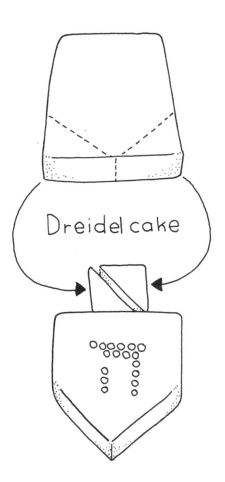

Dreidel cake

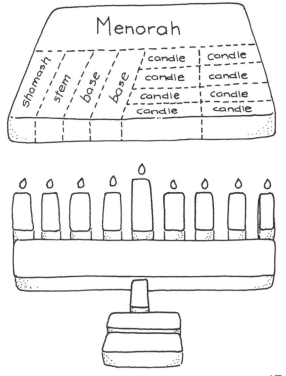

Menorah

CHANU-COOKIES

What You Need:

½ c. butter or margarine
1 c. sugar
1 tsp. vanilla
1 egg
1½ c. flour
1½ tsp. baking powder
¼ tsp. salt

---

2 bowls
Mixing spoon
Measuring cup and spoons
Pastry board
Spatula
Cookie sheet and potholder
Timer

What You Do:

1. Combine butter and sugar in a bowl, and mix until smooth. Add egg and vanilla and mix well.

2. Sift flour, baking powder, and salt into another bowl.

3. Add half the flour mixture to the butter mixture, and stir. Add the rest of the flour mixture. Add more flour if dough is too sticky.

4. Form dough into a ball and wrap in waxed paper. Refrigerate for at least an hour.

5. Preheat oven to 375°.

6. Roll out dough on floured board or table. Cut with Chanukah cookie cutters. If you don't have any, cut out cardboard dreidel and star shapes and use them as a guide to cut the dough. Place on ungreased cookie sheet and bake for 8-10 minutes.

Makes 3-4 dozen.

DRINKS

FRUIT SHAKE

What You Need:

1 c. vanilla or plain yogurt
1 c. milk
1 c. fresh or frozen fruit
  (banana, strawberries,
  peaches)
1 Tbsp. sugar or honey
  (optional)

Measuring cup and spoons
Blender
Knife and cutting board

What You Do:

1. Cut fruit into chunks.
2. Combine all ingredients in blender,
   and blend until smooth.

Serves 2-3

EGG CREAM

What You Need:

16 oz. bottle club soda, chilled
1 c. milk
¼ c. chocolate syrup

Glasses
Measuring cup and spoons
Spoon
Straws

What You Do:

1. Put 1 Tbsp. chocolate syrup and
   ¼ c. milk in each glass. Stir.
2. Fill slowly to the top with club soda.
3. Serve with straws.

   Serves 4

HOT COCOA

What You Need:

2 c. milk
2 heaping Tbsp. pre-sweetened
  cocoa
Marshmallows

Measuring cup and spoons
Pot and pot holder
Spoon
Mugs

What You Do:

1. Put 1 heaping Tbsp. of cocoa in each mug.
2. Pour milk into pot and warm over low heat. Do not boil.
3. Pour milk into mugs and stir. Top with marshmallows.

Serves 2

MULLED CIDER

What You Need:

1 quart apple cider
½ orange
10 whole cloves
4 cinnamon sticks

Knife and cutting board
Pot with cover and pot holder
Timer
Mugs

What You Do:

1. Pour cider into pot.

2. Push cloves into cut side of orange. Place orange in pot and cover. Mull the cider over low heat for one hour.

3. Pour into mugs. Serve with cinnamon stick straws.

Serves 4-6

PUNCH

What You Need:

1 quart ginger ale
1 quart fruit juice (orange, pine-apple, berry, or mixed fruit)
1 pint fruit sherbet or ices
1 orange
Ice cubes*

Punchbowl
Ladle
Cups
Knife and cutting board

What You Do:

1. Combine ginger ale, fruit juice, and sherbet in punchbowl and stir.

2. Slice orange into rounds and float on punch.

3. Add ice cubes and serve.

   Serves 8-10

*It's fun to make colored ice! You can freeze fruit juice or just add food coloring to water. You can also make one giant "cube" in a plastic bowl or jello mold.

CHANUKAH
PARTIES

CANDLELIGHT DINNER

MENORAH INVITATION

Fold an 8½ × 11″ sheet of paper in half lengthwise and cut into two pieces. Fold one piece in half, in half again, and in half a third time. Draw a candle, making sure that the base is attached along the folds (see diagram). Cut out and open carefully. Write your invitation along the base in bright colors. Refold and send in envelopes.

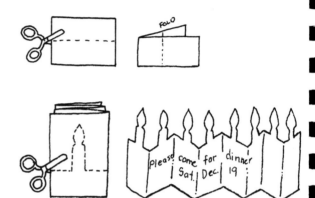

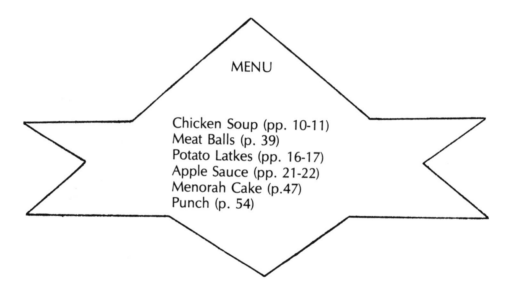

MENU

Chicken Soup (pp. 10-11)
Meat Balls (p. 39)
Potato Latkes (pp. 16-17)
Apple Sauce (pp. 21-22)
Menorah Cake (p.47)
Punch (p. 54)

DECORATION: PAPER CHAINS

Make a long paper chain and cut out Chanukah symbols to hang from your chain. Make dreidels, Maccabee soldiers, candles, and Chanukah gelt.

OPEN HOUSE

SHIELD INVITATION

Fold an 8½ × 11″ sheet of paper in half horizontally and cut into two pieces. Fold each piece in half. Draw a shield keeping the top along the fold line. Cut out. Decorate the front of your shield, and write the invitation inside.

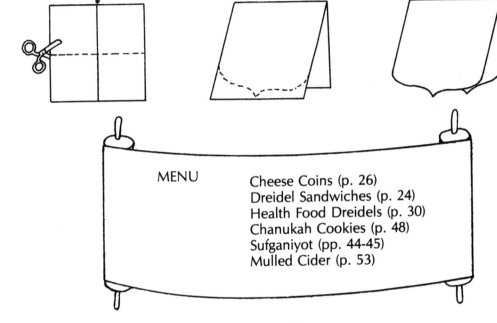

MENU
Cheese Coins (p. 26)
Dreidel Sandwiches (p. 24)
Health Food Dreidels (p. 30)
Chanukah Cookies (p. 48)
Sufganiyot (pp. 44-45)
Mulled Cider (p. 53)

DECORATION: DREIDEL GRAB-BAG CENTERPIECE

Buy or make small Chanukah gifts for each of your guests. These might include sewing kits, pens, magnets, mini-flashlights, key rings, gum, erasers. Tie a colorful piece of yarn around each gift. Put them in a paper bag with all the strings hanging out. Tie another string loosely around the bag. Cut out different colored dreidels and paste one to the end of each string. Use the bag as a centerpiece. At the end of the party, each guest may take home a surprise gift.

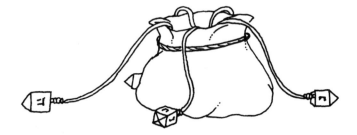

PAJAMA PARTY

PUZZLE INVITATION

Draw a dreidel on a piece of colored construction paper or cardboard, and cut it out. Write your party invitation, and decorate the dreidel. Outline puzzle piece shapes, and cut them out carefully. Send pieces in envelope. Your guests will have to put the puzzle together to find out about your party.

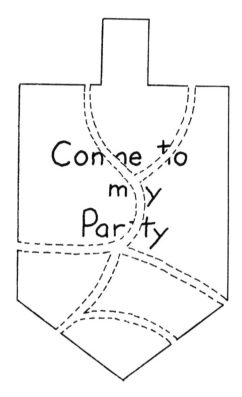

Come to my Party

MENU

Nighttime Snacks:

     Pizza Bagels (p. 29)
     Alef-Bet Pretzels (p. 46)
     Candy Dreidels (p. 42)
     Egg Creams (p. 51)

Brunch

     Cheese Latkes (p. 18)
     Candle Salad (p. 27)
     Winter Fruit Salad (p. 31)
     Sufganiyot (pp. 44-45)
     Hot Cocoa (p. 52)

DECORATION: SPINNING DREIDEL

Put two pieces of construction paper together, fold them in half, and draw half a dreidel shape along the fold. Cut them out. Slit each dreidel along the fold: one halfway from the top to the center, and the other halfway from the bottom to the center. Slide the two together through the slits. Punch a small hole in the top, and hang your spinning dreidels around the room. You may make spinning candles and stars the same way.

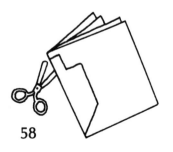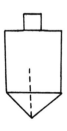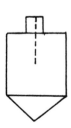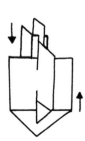

CHANUKAH
GAMES

DREIDEL

The most popular Chanukah game is dreidel. The dreidel is a spinning top. Its name in Yiddish means "turn." The Hebrew word for dreidel is *sevivon*.

There are four letters on the dreidel:

They stand for the words, *Nes Gadol Hayah Sham,* which means "A Great Miracle Happened There."

Dreidels in Israel have the letters:

They stand for the words, *Nes Gadol Hayah Poh,* which means "A Great Miracle Happened Here."

Here are the rules for playing dreidel:

Everyone starts with an equal number of pennies, nuts, raisins, or Chanukah gelt. Each player puts one of these in the middle. The first player spins the dreidel. If it lands on:

    Nun—the player does nothing
    Gimmel—the player takes everything in the middle
    Hey—the player takes half
    Shin—the player puts one in

An easy way to remember is:

    N = nothing
    G = get
    H = half
    SH = share

Before the next player spins, everyone puts another piece in the middle.

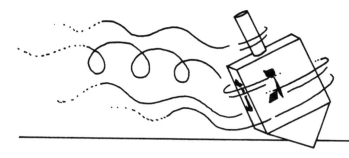

DREIDEL VARIATIONS

- See who can keep a dreidel spinning the longest. Time the spins with a stop watch.

- Try spinning the dreidel upside down.

- Let everyone spin a dreidel. Those whose dreidels land on the same letter get a point; the others lose. Play to a specified number of points.

- Hebrew letters stand for numbers: Nun is 50; Gimel is 3; Hey is 5; and Shin is 300. (On an Israeli dreidel, Pey is 80.) Take turns spinning the dreidel, and after each spin, record each player's score. See who can get to 1,000 first.

- Dreidel hunt: One player leaves the room while the others hide a dreidel. The player returns to hunt for the hidden dreidel, while the rest sing a Chanukah song. As the searcher comes closer to the hidden dreidel, the singing grows louder; as he or she moves away, the singing gets softer.

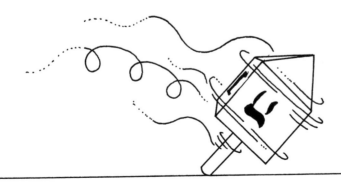

CHANUKAH BINGO

You will need:

Squares of cardboard or poster board (about 10 inches square)
Paper or index cards
Crayons, markers, ruler, scissors
Buttons or pennies
Shoe box

Rule each card into nine boxes to look like a Bingo card. Draw Chanukah symbols in each square. Make each card different. (Some ideas are King, Judah, Star of David, Menorah, Shield, Temple, Dreidel, Candle, Latkes, Jug of Oil.) You can use some of the same pictures on each card, but put them in different squares. Cut index cards or paper into small squares. Draw the same pictures or symbols on the smaller cards. Make sure you have a small card for each picture used on your Bingo cards. Put the small cards in a shoe box. One person is the caller. Everyone else has a large card. The caller picks a small card from the box, calls out the symbol, and whoever has that picture on his card, covers it with a button, penny, or small cardboard circle. The winner is the first person to complete a row of pictures, either across, down, or diagonally.

SUFGANIYOT ON A STRING

You Will Need:

1 donut for each player
1 foot-long piece of string for each donut

Tie a string around each donut. Each player must put the string in his mouth, and, at a signal, chew up the string until he or she reaches the donut. The first person to take a bite is the winner. Players must keep their hands behind their backs at all times.

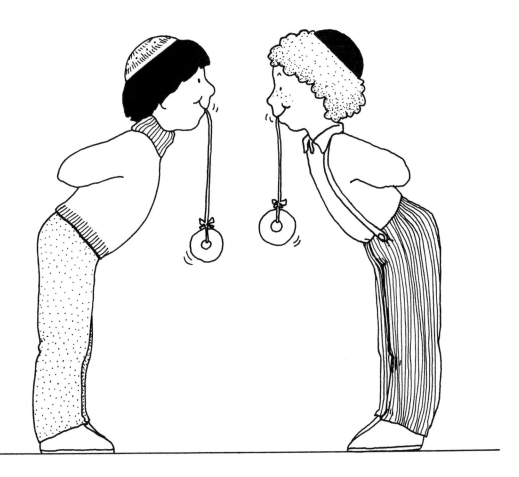

CHANUKAH GELT TREASURE HUNT

You Will Need:

Dozens of pennies or Chanukah gelt
Paper bag for each player

Hide the pennies or gelt around the house or party room. Give each player a bag. Set a time limit, and see who can collect the most gelt. Players get to keep their treasures.